HOMEWOOD PUBLIC LIBRARY

3 1311 00495 8322

W9-BRS-930

J
B
DRA

Drake

By Lynn Peppas

HOMEWOOD PUBLIC LIBRARY

MAR   2012

Crabtree Publishing Company

www.crabtreebooks.com

Crabtree Publishing Company
www.crabtreebooks.com

Author: Lynn Peppas
Publishing plan research and development:
  Sean Charlebois, Reagan Miller
  Crabtree Publishing Company
Project coordinator: Kathy Middleton
Photo research: Crystal Sikkens
Editor: Molly Aloian
Proofreader: Crystal Sikkens
Designer: Ken Wright
**Production coordinator and Prepress
  technician:** Ken Wright

Photographs:
Associated Press: pages 12, 21, 22
Getty Images: WireImage: page 24; AFP:
  page 25
Keystone Press: wenn.com: pages 9, 11, 26;
  Dane Andrew/KPA/Zuma: page 14; Russ
  Elliot/AdMedia: page 16; Paul Smith/
  Featureflash: page 17; MGM/Zuma/
  Entertainment Pictures: page 19;
  ZUMApress: page 27
Shutterstock: cover, pages 4, 5, 6, 7, 8, 10,
  13, 28
Wikimedia Commons: SimonP: page 15

Every effort has been made to trace copyright holders and to
obtain their permission for use of copyright material. The
authors and publishers would be pleased to rectify any error or
omission in future editions. All the Internet addresses given in
this book were correct at the time of going to press. The author
and publishers regret any inconvenience caused if addresses
have changed or sites have ceased to exist, but can accept no
responsibility for any such changes.

Library and Archives Canada Cataloguing in Publication

Peppas, Lynn
    Drake / Lynn Peppas.

(Superstars!)
Includes index.
Issued also in an electronic format.
ISBN 978-0-7787-7606-2 (bound).--ISBN 978-0-7787-7611-6 (pbk.)

    1. Drake, 1986- --Juvenile literature. 2. Rap musicians--
Canada--Biography--Juvenile literature. I. Title. II. Series:
Superstars! (St. Catharines, Ont.)

ML3930.D762P42 2011   j782.421649092   C2011-905251-2

Library of Congress Cataloging-in-Publication Data

Peppas, Lynn.
  Drake / by Lynn Peppas.
    p. cm. -- (Superstars!)
  Includes index.
  ISBN 978-0-7787-7606-2 (reinforced library binding : alk. paper) --
  ISBN 978-0-7787-7611-6 (pbk. : alk. paper) -- ISBN 978-1-4271-8852-6
  (electronic pdf) -- ISBN 978-1-4271-9755-9 (electronic html)
  1. Drake, 1986---Juvenile literature. 2. Rap musicians--United
States--Juvenile literature. I. Title. II. Series.

  ML3930.D73P46 2012
  782.421649092--dc23
  [B]
                                                    2011029842

Crabtree Publishing Company

www.crabtreebooks.com   1-800-387-7650

Printed in Canada/082011/MA20110714

Copyright © **2012 CRABTREE PUBLISHING COMPANY.** All rights reserved. No part of this publication may be reproduced,
stored in a retrieval system or be transmitted in any form or by any means, electronic, mechanical, photocopying, recording, or
otherwise, without the prior written permission of Crabtree Publishing Company. In Canada: We acknowledge the financial support of
the Government of Canada through the Canada Book Fund for our publishing activities.

Published in Canada
Crabtree Publishing
616 Welland Ave.
St. Catharines, ON
L2M 5V6

Published in the United States
Crabtree Publishing
PMB 59051
350 Fifth Avenue, 59th Floor
New York, New York 10118

Published in the United Kingdom
Crabtree Publishing
Maritime House
Basin Road North, Hove
BN41 1WR

Published in Australia
Crabtree Publishing
3 Charles Street
Coburg North
VIC 3058

CONTENTS

Words that are defined in the glossary are in
bold type the first time they appear in the text.

The Rap on Drake

Drake is a Canadian superstar. He started out as an actor on a Canadian television series called *Degrassi: The Next Generation*. In a few episodes of *Degrassi*, Drake's character, Jimmy Brooks, performs **freestyle** raps. Rap is a type of music where musicians quickly speak rhyming **lyrics** called a flow. In real life, Drake wrote rap lyrics and music in his spare time. He released his first **mixtape** on the Internet when he was 19 years old. Drake enjoyed acting, but he said that music is really where his heart is.

He Said It

"I just want to be like Drake—I just want to be me."
–In an interview for *ABC News*, July 2009

Not Your Typical Rapper

Many people say that Drake does not fit into the **typical** rapper stereotype. A stereotype is a particular image that people think of when talking about a group of people, such as rap artists. Rappers usually write lyrics that talk about social issues such as poverty, crime, or illegal drug use. Many rappers were raised in **underprivileged** neighborhoods that they often call "the hood." They write rap lyrics to talk about these issues because many have experienced them while growing up. They also rap about the expensive things they now own because of their musical success.

Drake's music is different because poverty, crime, and drugs weren't a part of his life growing up. Drake is a Jewish Canadian who was raised in a wealthy neighborhood in Toronto. Drake raps about what he knows instead. His songs are often about his newfound fame, or his past relationships with girlfriends. Another quality that sets him apart from other rappers is that he's **modest** and doesn't like to brag!

Rapping with the Superstars

Drake's music career got its biggest boost of success from other superstar rappers. Dwayne Carter who goes by the name, Lil Wayne, made the biggest change in Drake's music career as a rapper. Today, Drake works with many famous rappers such as Kanye West, and Eminem. He also writes songs for superstar musicians such as Dr. Dre and Alicia Keyes.

After hearing some of Drake's music, Lil Wayne immediately asked Drake to join him on tour. They also recorded a couple of songs together, such as "Ransom" and "I Want This Forever."

He Said It

"For anybody that doesn't believe in me, your favorite rappers do. They call me for **hooks**, features, and all that."

—In an interview in *XXL* Magazine, May 2010

Getting A Bad Rap

Rap lyrics often express emotion through strong language. Rap musicians are sometimes accused of writing lyrics that adults feel are **inappropriate** for young music listeners. This is true of all popular music, not just rap. Sometimes songs contain **profanity**, or swearing. Some rappers also write about subjects that may be upsetting. By law, CDs with adult language or subjects have an "Explicit Lyrics" warning. This label means that the words to songs on the CD are not considered appropriate for young listeners.

Edits are often made to songs so that they can be played on the radio. They do this by bleeping over swear words, or replacing them with other, less **offensive** ones. Download sites, such as iTunes, also feature different versions of the same song for listeners.

Drake helped write the hit song "Unthinkable" for Alicia Keyes.

7

School of Rap

Part of Drake's charm is his modest nature. Rap superstars are known for having big egos, which means they talk and act like they are the best. But Drake remains modest even though he's now a **hip-hop** superstar. He is modest enough to admit that he still has a lot to learn in making rap music. To learn more he studies the careers of other hip-hop superstars. He also studies other artists' music to try and improve upon his own style of rap music.

To help improve his own music, Drake watched other musicians perform live in concert, such as Jay-Z.

He Said It

"I can say I'm studying rap a lot more. I'm trying to get better so I hope that changes. I hope I get better on the next album, and better on the next album—that's the only thing I want to change."
—In an interview on 106KMEL, Summer 2010

Looking the Part of a Superstar

Drake has all the qualities of a male model, such as model-like height, slim body type, and great looks. Drake has modeled fashions for *GQ* magazine, and *Men's Fashion* magazine. Drake made it onto *GQ* magazine's Man of the Year list in 2010.

The 6'2" (188 cm) tall, brown-eyed entertainer is very "Hollywood" handsome and looks as good as he sounds. The clean-cut rapper is known for his sweet, **charismatic** smile, and beautiful, brown eyes.

He Said It

"People always have something to say about the way I look or the way I dress. People nitpick at my physical appearance more than my music, which is fine with me because when I look in the mirror, I know I'm not an unattractive person."
—In an interview for *Paper* Magazine, Summer 2010

Different Worlds

Drake's full name is Aubrey Drake Graham. As an actor, he goes by the name Aubrey Graham. As a musician, he uses the name Drake. He was born on Friday, October 24, 1986, in Toronto, Ontario, Canada. Toronto is the capital of Ontario, and has more people living there than any other city in Canada. More than two and a half million people live there today.

Parental Division

Drake's parents, Sandi and Dennis Graham, divorced when he was five years old. His father moved back to Memphis, Tennessee. Drake and his mom stayed in Toronto. His mother remained single, and Drake was an only child. Drake said his parents' split did affect him. He said he had to become a man very quickly so he could help look after his mom, whom he loves very much.

He Said It

"I love this city (Toronto) with my entire life."
–In a performance at his OVO concert in Toronto, August 2010

Drake's Mom

Drake and his mother, Sandi, have always had a very close, loving relationship. Sandi Graham is a Jewish Canadian. She supported the two of them in Toronto on her teacher's salary. Drake's mom was one of the most important people in his life. She remembers that Drake had his first guitar and microphone when he was just three years old.

Sandi recognized her son's talents early on in his life and signed him with a talent agency when he was just five years old. At the time, he did modeling. He also landed some roles in TV commercials. Sandi believed in keeping her young son busy and signed him up for team sports such as hockey.

And just as she took care of her son as a child growing up, Drake also takes care of his mom now that he's an adult. When Sandi was sick and needed an operation, Drake cancelled a part of his European tour and asked his fans to pray for her in the summer of 2010.

Drake and his mother, Sandi, pose together at the 2011 Juno Awards in Toronto, ON.

Mr. Emotional

Drake has said that he is a very emotional person. His mother thinks that his "softer" side comes from being raised in a female-run household by both herself and Drake's grandmother. She said that while Drake was growing they were "inseparable." Now Drake taps into his emotions to write honest and heartfelt lyrics for his songs.

Drake's sensitive side shines as he shows his love for his mother by giving her a kiss.

She Said It

"I always thought that there was something very different about this kid (Drake). When we had a piano at home, and I would come home with my nursery rhymes—Aubrey as a three-year-old would take the lyrics and change them. I realized that other kids just didn't do that."

—Sandi Graham in an interview from "Degrassi Un-Scripted"

Drake's Dad

Drake's father, Dennis Graham, who is African-American, is a musician. He played the drums with rock and roll legend Jerry Lee Lewis. As a young boy, Drake often spent summer vacations in Memphis with his dad. Drake described his dad as someone who was "more like a little brother."

EARLY INTEREST

When Drake was 16 years old, his father served time in prison. Drake would keep in touch with his dad by phone. The man who shared a cell with his father was into rap music. Drake got to know him and began to write his own rap lyrics so they could rap back and forth on the phone.

Jerry Lee Lewis is best known for his song "Great Balls of Fire." Drake's father played drums with Lewis.

He Said It

"My Dad had a lot to do with my music. My Dad is very musically gifted. ...I get my charm from my father if I do have any charm at all. ...Everything good in life I get from my mom. The desire to be intelligent, kind, caring, the fact that I just want to love somebody for real."

—In an interview for MTV.ca/MTV2 "Better Than Good Enough"

Music Talent Runs in the Family

Drake and his father aren't the only ones in the family who are musically talented. Drake's uncles, Mabon "Teenie" Hodges and Larry Graham, are both professional musicians, too. Teenie plays lead guitar for other musicians such as Cat Power. He's co-written famous songs such as "Take Me to the River," with soul singer, Al Green. Drake's uncle, Larry Graham is a professional bass guitar player who has worked with Prince, and Sly and the Family Stone.

Larry Graham was honored with a Innovator of Rock Award at the 2003 California Music Awards.

Drake's School Days

As a young boy, Drake went to Forest Hill Junior and Senior Public School in Toronto. He then went on to attend the local public high school, Forest Hill Collegiate Institute. Drake said he never felt like he fit in with the rich, white kids there. He dropped out of high school after having an argument with his history teacher.

Drake isn't proud of the fact that he didn't finish high school, especially since his mom was a teacher. He says he plans on graduating sometime in the future so he can show his diploma to his mom.

Drake attended this high school, but unfortunately never received his diploma.

He Said It

"I went to a Jewish school where nobody understood what it was like to be black and Jewish. ...But the same kids that made fun of me are super proud (of me) now. And they act as if nothing happened."
–In a magazine interview, June 18, 2010

15

Big Breaks for Drake

In 2001, when he was just 14 years old, Drake got his first big break in acting. He got the part of Jimmy Brooks in a Canadian television teen drama called *Degrassi High: The Next Generation*. Drake loved acting in the show, but there was another calling that he couldn't ignore. Drake started to make music, too. By the time his role on *Degrassi* ended, his music career really began to take off.

Drake poses with some of his cast members from *Degrassi High: The Next Generation*.

Degrassi High: The Next Generation

Aubrey Graham's character on *Degrassi* was a rich kid named Jimmy Brooks who played basketball . He was in more than 140 episodes of the popular Canadian teen drama.

In season four on the show, Jimmy is shot in the back by another student named Rick. He survives the shooting, but loses the ability to walk and has to use a wheelchair.

On the show, he discovers his talent for rap when he freestyles over a song sung by another *Degrassi* character named Ashley Kerwin. Aubrey's *Degrassi* days ended in 2009 when his character graduated from high school.

Drake attends the 2005 Teen Choice Awards where *Degrassi* wins for "Choice Summer Series."

He Said It

"Degrassi was a stepping stone. It was why people saw my face. ..."
—On Notable Interviews, December 7, 2007

The Renaissance

In 2004, when Drake was 17 years old, he joined a band called The Renaissance. Their music was a mix of Rhythm & Blues (R&B) and hip hop. Not long after he had joined, his manager phoned to tell him he was being thrown out of the group. They told him that they didn't think, "music was his calling." Drake said he was "heartbroken" over it, but he never gave up, obviously!

IN THE BEGINNING

Drake was inspired to become an actor because of his idol Denzel Washington. He started out his acting career by doing TV commercials for companies such as Sears, Toys "R" Us, and the GMC car company.

Room for Improvement

Even while he was working as an actor, Drake was busy making music in his spare time. His very first mixtape was called *Room for Improvement*. He worked with other musicians such as R&B singer, Trey Songz on the mixtape. Drake released it as a free download on his MySpace account in 2006.

He Said It

"Not only (was leaving acting) a big decision—it was a risk. Acting was something I was established in. And hip hop was like, a lot of people didn't get it. …But I just loved (music) that much. I really believed in my talent…"

—In an interview with SB.TV, June 2010

Busy on the Big Screen

Aubrey landed a small role in the movie *Charlie Bartlett*, which was released in August of 2007. He also appeared in the television movie *Degrassi Spring Break Movie* in 2008. He got small roles on Canadian television shows, such as *Being Erica*, while working on the *Degrassi* set and making music, too.

In 2009, Drake had to make a serious decision as to what career path he wanted to follow, music or acting. Drake's character on *Degrassi* was graduating, and therefore his acting job was ending. Drake decided to put acting on hold and try a career in music instead.

ANTON YELCHIN HOPE DAVIS KAT DENNINGS AND ROBERT DOW

CHARLIE BARTLETT

people like you ARE THE REASON people like me NEED MEDICATION.

www.CharlieBartlett-TheMovie.com

Drake played the character A/V Jones in the movie *Charlie Bartlett*.

Comeback Season

Drake released his second mixtape, called *Comeback Season*, in 2007. On it was the song, "Replacement Girl," that featured R&B singer, Trey Songz. The song became so popular that it became Drake's first single and the music video for it was played on BET (Black Entertainment Television). *Comeback Season* was also a free download mixtape that Drake released on his MySpace account.

DRIZZY DRAKE

Lil Wayne gave Drake a new nickname: Drizzy. Lil Wayne sometimes goes by the nickname: Weezy. He gave Drake a nickname that was much like his own.

He Said It

"One of the greatest things I love about Wayne is that he always encourages me, and everyone else in Young Money, to be myself. He actually asked me to please never get a tattoo. He really was like, 'please never stop smiling, please never get a tattoo, just be yourself. …He urges me to do the music I want to do, dress the way I want to dress, do the videos I want to shoot, and he's an amazing mentor and boss to have."

—In an interview on *Jimmy Kimmel Live*, 2010

Lil Wayne

A friend of Drake's, named Jazz Prince, brought Drake's mixtape, *Comeback Season*, to Lil Wayne to listen to. After hearing a few songs on the CD, Lil Wayne phoned Drake. Drake got the call while getting his hair cut at the barber's in Toronto. Lil Wayne invited him to fly from Toronto to Houston, Texas, where Lil Wayne was on tour. Drake first met Lil Wayne in his tour bus where the rap superstar was getting a tattoo done. Drake went on tour with Lil Wayne. During this time they wrote and recorded songs together, such as "I Want This Forever."

Drake's friendship with Lil Wayne changed his music career almost overnight. Suddenly other superstar hip-hop singers such as Jay-Z and Kanye West wanted to work with Drake on music projects, too.

Drake and Lil Wayne teamed up again to perform at the 2009 BET Awards Show.

Drake's Climb to Fame

Drake knew the time was right to make a move to music when his role on *Degrassi: The Next Generation* ended. He had met important people in the music industry and was ready to record another mixtape. It was this mixtape that launched Drake's music career from little-known rapper to superstar.

So Far Gone

Drake released his third mixtape, *So Far Gone*, in February of 2009. In the fall of 2009, Drake released *So Far Gone* as an **EP**. The EP had five songs from the original mixtape, plus two new songs. In its first week of sales it sold 73,000 copies and became the fifth-best-selling rap album of 2009. The EP went gold, which means it sold more than 500,000 copies. The EP also won a 2010 Canadian music Juno Award for Rap Recording of the Year.

Drake not only won the award for Rap Recording of the Year at the 2010 Juno Awards, he also won New Artist of the Year.

Best I Ever Had

The first single from the EP, "Best I Ever Had," became a Billboard Top 10 hit and was named the Hot Rap Song of 2009. At the 2009 Grammy Awards, "Best I Ever Had" got Drake nominations for Best Rap Solo Performance and Best Rap Song.

De-Toured

Drake injured his knee while playing basketball before he went on a U.S. tour in the summer of 2009. On July 31, 2009, in New Jersey, he fell while onstage performing his song, "The Best I Ever Had," with Lil Wayne. He was in a lot of pain and stagehands had to carry him offstage. On September 8, 2009, he had surgery in Canada to correct the torn **ligament** in his knee.

WHAT A DEAL!

After a bidding war with a couple of different labels, Drake signed on with Lil Wayne's record company and received quite a good deal. He received a $2 million up-front advance and all his publishing rights.

He Said It

"It was bad. (My knee) buckled, popped. I was down. I remember slapping the ground. I couldn't believe it. I saw the lights coming down. [And I was thinking] 'Did I just fall?' I was in so much pain then that I didn't care at the time."
—In an interview for MTV News, August 17, 2009

More Than A Game for Drake

Drake recorded his next hit song, "Forever," in August of 2009. Drake's song features verses from Eminem, Kanye West, and Lil Wayne. It was released on the soundtrack for the movie called *More Than a Game*. Eminem later released it on his album, *Relapse: Refill*.

"Forever" became the number one hit on the Hot Billboard Rap songs chart in November of 2009. Drake performed the song with Lil Wayne and Eminem at the 52rd Grammy Awards show. Drake's superstar status was climbing to the top and he hadn't even released his **debut** album yet!

Drake, Eminem, and Lil Wayne perform "Forever" at the 2010 Grammy Awards.

He Said It

"...Coming up with a verse is probably one of the best feelings in my life, period. ...I remember the night I came up with the "Forever" verse and finished typing in the last word, 'cause I write on my phone. ...It's fun to me, man. I love it."
—In an interview for *XXL* magazine, May 2010

Drake's Romance Department

Drake isn't usually the kiss-and-tell type. But a few of his past girlfriends such as Canadian pop singer Keshia Chante have made it into verses of his songs. Drake's song, "Deceiving" talks about his past relationships with Keshia when he was 16 years old.

Drake's most famous romantic link was with hip-hop singer, Rihanna, in May of 2009. The two were spotted together kissing at a nightclub. They both said they were just good friends. Later, Rihanna admitted that she and Drake did have a short romance. Rihanna featured Drake in her hit song and video, "What's My Name," where Drake plays her steamy love-interest.

Drake and Rihanna perform the hit song "What's My Name" at the 53rd Annual Grammy Awards.

Drake and Nicki

Drake raps about his love for fellow hip-hop singer, Nicki Minaj, in his song, "Miss Me." The two also got together for one of Nicki Minaj's songs, "Moment 4 Life." In this song, Drake raps about he and Nicki getting married. But the two have never admitted that they are romantically involved outside of their lyrics.

Drake keeps his love life a secret from his fans. The one woman in Drake's life he openly confesses his love for is his mother, Sandi. In fact, he even brought his mom as his date for the 2010 and 2011 Grammy Awards show.

Nicki Minaj teams up with Drake to perform her song "Moment 4 Life."

Thank Me Later

The pressure was on for Drake to produce a superstar **debut** album after having so much success without one. Drake's full-length debut album finally came out on June 15, 2010. It was titled, *Thank Me Later*. Superstar rappers such as Kanye West, Timbaland, and Lil Wayne, joined on different songs on the album.

Drake said he called the album *Thank Me Later* because of the pressure he felt making the album. He wasn't sure if people would like it. He also said he felt rushed to make the album. He called his upcoming album *Take Care* because he took more time making the album.

During its first week of sales, *Thank Me Later* sold more copies than any other album in the U.S., according to the U.S. Billboard 200 chart. The album went platinum, which means it sold over one million copies in both Canada and the United States.

Drake performed songs from his *Thank Me Later* album on his tour Light Dreams & Nightmares.

He Said It

"I feel like I did a good job on Thank Me Later, *but I feel like I could get better. I could just tell better stories. I'm watching people speak, watching other people's careers, watching friends, watching lovers, everything. Just watching. I'm willing to learn with my eyes open."*
—In an interview for *Men's Fashion* magazine, Fall 2010

OVO Fest

Drake started his own annual hip-hop festival in 2010. Named after his entertainment company, October's Very Own, the first OVO Fest in August 2010 featured surprise appearances by Eminem and Jay-Z. At OVO Fest 2011, Lil Wayne and Stevie Wonder performed.

Star Status

Drake's at work on his next album, *Take Care*. It is due out on Drake's 25th birthday, October 24, 2011. Over the summer of 2011, Drake released three songs on his blog before the official release date: "Dreams Money Can Buy," "Marvin's Room," and "Headlines," which became the first single available for play on the radio. He hosted Canada's Juno Awards show in 2011 and is looking at upcoming movie roles. He has joked that he would be perfect to play the role of President Barack Obama in a movie because he resembles the American politician.

Drake is one of the hardest-working rap stars and actors in the entertainment business. He even raps about it in his hit song, "Unstoppable:" "My name is Drizzy and I ain't perfect, But I work hard so I deserve it…" The hard-working actor from Canada who dreamed of making a career in music is making a superstar splash on the rap music scene worldwide.

Timeline

October 24, 1986: Aubrey Drake Graham is born in Toronto, Ontario, Canada.

2001: Drake lands the part of Jimmy Brooks in the teen drama *Degrassi High: The Next Generation*.

2004: Drake joins a band called The Renaissance.

2006: Drake releases his first mixtape called *Room for Improvement* on his MySpace account.

2007: Drake gets a small role in a feature film called *Charlie Bartlett*.

2007: Drake releases his second mixtape called *Comeback Season* on his MySpace account.

2008: Drake appears on the television movie, *Degrassi Spring Break Movie*.

February 2009: Drake releases his third mixtape called *So Far Gone*.

Fall 2009: *So Far Gone* is released as an EP.

2009: Drake's hit single, "Best I Ever Had," was named Billboard's Hot Rap Song of 2009.

August 1, 2010: Drake holds the first annual OVO Fest in Toronto.

January 31, 2010: Drake, Eminem, and Lil Wayne perform "Forever" at the Grammy Awards show.

April 2010: Drake wins Junos for New Artist of the Year and Rap Recording of the Year for *So Far Gone*.

April 2010: Drake begins his Away From Home Tour across North America.

June 15, 2010: Drake's debut album, *Thank Me Later*, is released in the United States.

September 2010: Drake begins his Light Dreams and Nightmares Tour in the United States.

March 2011: Drake hosts 2011 Juno Awards show.

July 31, 2011: Drake headlines the second OVO Fest.

Summer 2011: Drake releases three new songs from his next album, *Take Care*, on his blog.

October 24, 2011: Official release date of Drake's second album *Take Care*.

Glossary

charismatic Having a magnetic quality that makes people like you

debut The first of something

EP A musical recording that is longer than a single, or one-song recording, but not as long as a full-length album

freestyle To create a rap verse in the moment or on the spot

hip hop African-American art, music, and culture. Rap is one style of hip-hop music.

hook In music, a hook is a catchy musical bar, or phrase, that draws in listeners.

inappropriate Not suitable for some listeners

ligament Strands of tissue in your body that help to connect bones and cartilages at joints or keep organs in place

lyrics The words to a song

mixtape A homemade CD that may contain remixes of other artists' songs

modest Dislikes to call attention to oneself, not showy

offensive Something that causes anger, insult, or displeasure

profanity Words considered to be offensive

typical Having the same qualities as others in a group

underprivileged Not given the same advantages or opportunities as most others have

Find Out More

Websites

Drake's official site
www.drakeofficial.com/

Biography for Aubrey Drake Graham
http://www.imdb.com/name/nm1013044/bio

Crabtree Publishing has tried to provide websites that are suitable for all audiences. However, we accept no responsibility for any explict or inappropriate materials that may be found on the above websites.

About the Author
Lynn Peppas is a writer of children's nonfiction books. She has always been a bookworm and grew up reading all the books she could. She feels fortunate to have been able to combine her love of reading and her love of kids into a career. Her work in children's publishing is a dream-job come true.

Index